LIFE EXTRAORDINARY AND SOBER

LIFE EXTRAORDINARY AND SOBER

PETE LOTTERHOS

LIFE EXTRAORDINARY AND SOBER
Print ISBN: 9798395816061
Ebook available.
Copyright © Pete Lotterhos, 2023

Acknowledgements

Several people on my team, friends, and experts assisted in the development and writing of this book. I acknowledge the group of people who are committed to me and sharing with the world the type of insight that sets in motion possibility over order, authenticity over self-righteousness.

Nathan Barnes, Paul Kandarian, and Christina Roye: thank you for your commitment to helping me bridge the gap between my thoughts and the expression of my thoughts in text. Writing with you is an absolute pleasure.

Special thanks to my support group. You have inspired my personal transformation and helped me embrace life extraordinary and sober.

Debralee Cartolano, thank you for seeing my potential and showing me what is truly possible for people who have chosen recovery!

Contents

Glossary of Terms

Absolute Accountability: The practice of taking full responsibility for generating or creating one's life and the impact that one has on others.

Addiction: Compulsive behavior that may include substance abuse, dysfunctional behavior, and duplication of past emotional trauma.

Choice: The act of creating a new, extraordinary life out of possibility.

Connection: An interaction that leaves each person feeling inspired to create an extraordinary life.

Conscious Creation: The act of designing one's life intentionally rather than generating an environment based on reactions to unresolved past pain. Conscious creation is characterized by the freedom to dream, strive, and achieve.

Context: The frame of mind that either generates or creates an environment.

Decision: *Mind Dynamics* distinguishes the words *decide* and *choose*. A *decision* murders possibility. The word *decide* employs *-cide*, from Latin *to cut*, like suicide, the murder of oneself; homicide, the murder of someone else; or regicide, the murder of a king. The word *choice* is creative: it implies that we are selecting from other possibilities.

Emotional Addiction: A chemical dependency that drives people to generate an environment that recreates in their present circumstances the feeling of painful emotions that they previously experienced.

Emotional Relapse: Any return to generating present behaviors from reactions to painful emotions.

Emotional Integrity: A completely neutral state of being that gives us space to fully accept our emotions and take responsibility for the results that we generate or create.

Emotional Sobriety: The commitment to consciously creating our lives rather than reacting to our emotions.

Environment: The entire framework in which one operates.

Life Extraordinary and Sober: A new life of sobriety that exists out of self-awareness, creating connections with friends and family members, overcoming depression and anxiety, improving health, and achieving peak performance in the workplace.

Generate: The act of producing results in life based on reactions to unresolved past pain and circumstances.

Radical Honesty: The choice to share the thinking, feeling, and perceiving that we have about ourselves and others that are normally repressed.

Recovery Community: Everyone involved in the recovery process for substance and behavioral disorders: those seeking treatment and their friends, families, healthcare providers, and businesses that support recovery.

Relapse: *Mind Dynamics* defines relapse as any return to substance use and addictive behaviors.

Sobriety: Total abstinence from addictive chemicals and behaviors.

Substances: *Mind Dynamics* offers treatment for the ten classes of substances described in the DSM-5-TR: alcohol, caffeine, cannabis, hallucinogens, inhalants, opioids, sedatives, hypnotics or anxiolytics, and stimulants (including amphetamine-type substances, cocaine, and other stimulants).

Substance Use Disorder: *Mind Dynamics* follows the eleven criteria for substance use disorder as described in the DSM-5-TR. A person may be diagnosed with SUD if they meet at least two of the following criteria: using larger amounts for a longer time than intended, failed repeated attempts to manage use, have cravings or urges to use, failing to manage responsibilities at home or work due to use, continuing to use when it causes problems, building tolerance, and experiencing withdrawal.

Transparency: The choice to bring our hidden emotions out into the open.

Preface

WE USE LANGUAGE TO CREATE OUR LIVES. Our background and experience give us vocabulary to create inner conversations that shape our reality. For example, people who live on the street and people who were born with a silver spoon in their mouths will talk about their circumstances using different vocabularies. Each person's perspective will be distinct, and that distinction lives in language.

Please utilize the glossary that we have provided. Some of the words that we use to transform the conversation about recovery are defined. We define our inner lives using language that determines our external results.

Enjoy the Journey!

Pete Lotterhos
President
Mind Dynamics, LLC
Plainville, CT

Introduction

MIND DYNAMICS IS AN OUTPATIENT CLINIC and sober community. We are located in Plainville, CT, and we take an educational approach to recovery from substance use disorder, behavioral addiction, and emotional addiction. *Mind Dynamics* offers an evidence-based partial hospitalization program (PHP), intensive outpatient program (IOP), and outpatient program (OP) for substance use disorder and behavioral addiction, with additional child and family therapy. Our Sober Community is a continuum of care for those seeking additional support. *Mind Dynamics* utilizes LEAP: *Life Extraordinary Approach Process*, an educational process that includes our Life Skills Seminar Series and Empowerment Training to address emotional addiction. Our invitation to life extraordinary extends to all persons of any age seeking sobriety, along with family, friends, businesses, and churches—the entire community that is committed to empowering long-term recovery. Everyone is included.

Mind Dynamics explores what is possible for people in the recovery community who are committed to transforming their capacity to create their lives.

Each human being is given the opportunity to create their lives. When we were children, we looked at the world through the lens of endless possibilities. That was before trauma and social criticism sabotaged our creative nature. Most of us, in time, will exchange our creative potential for fitting in and feeling safe. We begin to use our pain to generate our lives, and we unintentionally limit our capacity to dream and stifle our ability to achieve. We unintentionally imprison ourselves in a vicious cycle, generating our future out of reactions to past painful experiences like rejection, abandonment, and neglect. Substance use disorder and all its devastation thrive in this dysfunctional environment. *Mind Dynamics* explores what is possible for people in the recovery community who are committed to transforming their capacity to create their lives.

Mind Dynamics works with people who choose recovery and their families to create life extraordinary and sober. *Mind Dynamics* also partners with peer groups and businesses in the recovery community to engage in a new conversation that will transform the future of recovery. In this book, we identify the breakdown that hinders long-term recovery as *sobriety while sabotaging choice* and propose the language of a life extraordinary and sober.

Mind Dynamics navigates the creative process to access the power of choice as a way to free ourselves from self-imposed limitations to achieve life extraordinary and sober.

Our vision for recovery goes beyond establishing physical sobriety using our PHP/IOP/OP and therapy programs. We understand that the individual in recovery can be sober but depressed, anxious, overwhelmed, or feel dead inside, all of which can lead to relapse and dysfunction. LEAP focuses on our ability to envision and achieve in our lives. Through the development of self-awareness, we come face-to-face with our emotional trauma, such as rejection, criticism, and abandonment. This process provides the opportunity for personal transformation. *Mind Dynamics* invites the recovery community to access the power of choice to break through self-imposed limitations to achieve a life extraordinary and sober.

Mind Dynamics teaches people how to build a new environment that transforms the future of their recovery. We are proposing a new framework from which to view recovery rather than providing a different or "best practice." In our facility, we offer 12-Steps, cognitive behavioral therapy, and Smart Recovery as resources that drive sobriety. We are not trying to change these external processes. *Mind Dynamics* is committed to addressing the real issue: our internal relationship with our 'self.' We focus on practices that people can add to conventional recovery programs to break through self-imposed barriers, achieve long-term recovery, and create a healthy, productive, and successful life.

The *Mind Dynamics* Sober Community and LEAP offer space for self-exploration that inspires people with substance use disorder and their families to embrace the power of choice in their lives. We operate from the position that each of us has the power to transform the quality of our lives. Our process begins by examining the construct in which most people operate: we do not have the self-awareness necessary for choice.

We invite the recovery community to answer the following questions of themselves:

- Do I feel overworked and overwhelmed?
- Do I struggle with depression or anxiety?
- Do I let my fears dictate my behaviors?
- Do I feel empty inside?
- Do I help others at the cost of my own emotional well-being?
- No matter what I have, do I still want or 'need' more?

If our answer is yes to any one of these questions, then we are probably generating our lives out of the same unresolved trauma, pain, and fear that produces addictive behaviors. The recovery community must address their own unresolved trauma, pain, and fear; otherwise, we will be unable to develop the capacity for choice and sabotage our future. While we may feel that we are doing our best to help ourselves and others, we will continue to produce emotional disconnection, inauthenticity, and juvenile behaviors that enable relapse and death. We blindly walk into a future that recreates our past pain when we unintentionally make decisions based on reactions to our past trauma.

The extraordinary does not come from the world that exists but from the world that does not exist.

To establish a new realm of possibility for recovery, we must be willing to explore our relationship to what is possible. Are we, the recovery community, willing to explore ourselves, not to find an answer or the "right action," but rather to unveil what is truly possible for ourselves and for the people we love who struggle with substance use and behavioral disorders? The extraordinary does not come from the world that exists but from the world that does not exist. This construct, creating something from nothing, speaks to the inspiring position that the recovery community can bring into being: a future characterized by a life extraordinary and sober.

Chapter 1: Exploring the Self

MIND DYNAMICS USES A FUTURE-FIRST APPROACH that has been changing lives and improving companies for the past 20 years. We have discovered through our work that the same breakdown that causes people to generate unfulfilling lives also causes corporations to underperform. The companies that preceded *Mind Dynamics* (*Synergy, Next Level Management,* and *Transformational Mind Dynamics*) and my books (*You Got that, Cindy?,* 2015 and *The 5 Principles of Coaching in Management,* 2018) have focused on what makes the most significant difference: the transformation of the *self.* The self is the aspect of us that is free to enjoy each moment before the ego hijacks our capacity to choose. The self is perfect, whole, and complete—it is free and alive. A person's relationship with the self has the power to make the biggest difference for an individual's life and a corporation's bottom line. This means that there is no 'right' employee or manager. Your child or spouse is not the issue. The issue is your relationship with your self.

I chose to participate in Mind Dynamics's seminar series after I heard a few people talking about their positive results. I went into it looking for help managing my anger. I went in with an open mind—a positive attitude—but never thought it would actually work. I've struggled with my anger for a lifetime. I came to see that I created my anger; it wasn't something that was happening to me. I feel free. It truly enhanced my own recovery, opening up new ideas, and giving me a new perspective on life in general. I was also able to increase the love and connection with my wife. – Mikey Cat.

Families and corporations are struggling to create quality results. Families are looking for love and connection, and corporations are looking for increased profitability, but the breakdown is the same: everyone is neglecting their power of choice. Whether *Mind Dynamics* is working with an individual or a corporation, our process provides each person the opportunity to explore their choices and the impact that their choices have on the future. In my book, *The 5 Principles of Coaching in Management*, I explore how a business executive, Wally, transformed his company's profitability by accessing personal accountability. Wally had to understand that he was holding his teams back by creating an environment where they needed to hide and defend themselves, which sabotaged their performance. As Wally learned how to take responsibility for his team's performance, the freedom that he created within himself empowered his teams to explore new behaviors that produced outstanding results for the company. A change in profitability was not caused by implementing expensive training programs, hiring new management, or buying new software: Wally's teams felt inspired to achieve.

The environment that we operate from in our schools, families, and support groups often makes it difficult to comprehend the impact that we have on others.

Similarly, in *You Got that, Cindy?*, Cindy (short for Cinderella) had to come to grips with the reality that had to take responsibility for creating her quality of life. Her circumstances were not created by her husband, the loss of her parents, or her evil stepsisters. It was not her past trauma that created her behavior. She had unintentionally used pain from her past to rationalize her behavior: self-medicating with pills and ignoring the root of her depression and anxiety. Before learning how to take responsibility for her decisions, she generated her behavior based on reactions to her feelings. As she developed the capacity to choose, she was able to create her life consciously. Her circumstances did not change; she changed her relationship with herself and created a new future.

We have found that the breakdown in life is not with the people in our lives or the organization's teams; the issue is the environment that we generate holds no space for people to be absolutely accountable for their choices. The environment that we operate from in our schools, families, and support groups often makes it difficult to recognize the impact that we have on others. This is why people give up their power to choose, operate from fear, and hope for the best. Our inability to grasp that we are generating our future from fear-based reactions sabotages our capacity to experience the present moment.

The breakdown is not "out there" but "in here."

Mind Dynamics is focused on the self's capacity to create future results consciously. We explore how our choices are made instead of worrying about the 'right' choice. A new future that includes sobriety, a healthy marriage, or financial freedom can only be created out of exploring how we generated the present dysfunction. We have worked with many families that are distracted by superficial issues like weight loss, status, and political theater; they cannot identify the real breakdown. Similarly, we have worked with business owners and managers that are focused on hiring the 'right' people, decreasing the time to train their teams, and increasing sales performance; they are unwilling to explore who they are in the matter. The break-down is not "out there" but "in here." This means that the most significant driver of long-term recovery exists within the individual's capacity to create. The pivotal position is account-ability: the act of taking ownership of one's life rather than placing blame on others.

The tools that we use to construct our environment—our thinking, feeling, speaking, and perceiving—will be hi-jacked by our past until we are empowered with the capacity to choose. Our past wounds will determine the quality of our interactions, how we interpret the world around us, the emo-tions we experience, and the language we use. This self-gener-ated narrative is what we use to generate our lives, which consequently is our future. Who we believe we are on the in-side generates who we are on the outside. If we are willing to examine our relationships, both personal and professional, we come face to face with a reflection of ourselves and the impact we have on others. For example, the wife has the opportunity to realize that the complaints she has about her husband can be a reflection of her inability to manage boundaries, and the business owner can recognize that they are hiring submissive employees out of their need for control.

> Nothing new or inspiring will occur until we realize that each individual is responsible for every breakdown in their life.

Without developing our capacity to choose, our future reality will be a reflection of our past pain. For example, parents will unintentionally turn their children into living representations of their own unresolved wounds. Diane was raised by an angry, self-absorbed father. She will raise angry, self-absorbed children by criticizing their choices and not managing boundaries until she addresses the truth about what drives her behavior. Managers like Dave who oversee several teams will continue to build an environment that enables poor performance—no matter who they hire—until they examine their own inability to be empathic. Of course, both Diane and Dave believe they are doing their best. The problem is families and business owners are being reactive to their emotions instead of proactive, recreating the pain from their past instead of choosing a productive future. Nothing new or inspiring will occur for Diane or Dave until they realize that each individual is responsible for every breakdown in their life.

The Recovery Community

The recovery community faces the same breakdown as families and businesses. Those who facilitate recovery are producing a culture that is defined by childhood trauma. We are seeing that sobriety generated out of unresolved emotional pain leads to relapse. For example, Chris may choose sobriety, but he is at serious risk of relapse if the cause of his addiction—in many cases, childhood trauma—is not addressed. Families who want to support their loved ones who choose recovery will enable disconnection unless they confront unresolved pain. Relapse and broken relationships thrive in a recovery environment where the primary objective is establishing sobriety, not developing the capacity to create a new future. Chris can access his unlimited potential and thrive in the face of adversity.

Without a robust continuum of care, conventional treatments are producing *sobriety while sabotaging choice*; Chris lacks the capacity to choose consciously, and those facilitating his recovery do not envision what is possible in life beyond sobriety. No one in Chris's life has access to the extraordinary. However honorable, the aim of conventional programs is to help Chris shift from being sick to healthy, producing a limited future.

It's time for people who think they are broken to realize that they have the capacity to transform.

Mind Dynamics is committed to teaching the recovery world how to create an environment that drives long-term sobriety by shifting the focus from sickness to inspiration. Instead of focusing on the notion that Chris did something wrong, we can acknowledge existing capabilities. For example, we can build on the obsessive nature that drives Chris's addictive behavior rather than insisting on change. This approach transforms the perspective of recovery. Furthermore, everyone involved in Chris's recovery effort is full of potential with an ability to achieve the extraordinary.

We can learn how to shift out of fear and into love by leveraging what empowers our ability to focus and achieve results in the face of pain and resistance. For example, athletes like Michael Jordan and scientists like Stephen Hawking are well-known for obsessing over their craft to create breakthrough results that are empowering, supportive, and rewarding. Their ability to focus makes a difference, creates healthy results, and generates possibility for the world, while Chris's obsession with alcohol or other substances can destroy his life and the lives of his loved ones. Chris, his family, and those who facilitate his recovery have the opportunity to shift the context in which they view recovery to transform what's possible for people who choose sobriety. It's time for people who think they are broken to realize that they have the capacity to transform. Everyone can create inspiring results by harnessing their pre-existing power to obsessively focus their attention on consciously designing their life.

The individual struggling with sobriety and their loved ones must embrace their innate capacity to create their lives consciously.

Mind Dynamics has identified the breakdown that is occurring in families, the corporate world, and the recovery community. People are being reactive to their past wounds and recreate them in their relationships, businesses, and recovery. Just like Diane, who generated an environment for her kids in a way that recreated her painful experiences with her father, Dave generated unproductive teams to duplicate his past pain. In both circumstances, determining the relationship with the self is the key. The self holds all the power to transform the future quality of life for Daine and Dave. For Chris, the person who chose recovery, the environment that drives *sobriety by sabotaging choice* must be explored in order to produce a future that is characterized by long-term sobriety, financial freedom, and healthy relationships. The recovery world must give human beings the opportunity to transform; otherwise, they will continue to recreate past pain as their future. Just like Diane and Dave, Chris and his family must embrace their innate capacity to create their lives consciously. This means that the self must go through whatever it has to go through to come to the other side, trusting that it has the power to create life extraordinary and sober.

Transforming the Future of Recovery

Mind Dynamics's educational process shifts the focus of recovery from the management of Chris's outer disease to addressing the inner breakdown of everyone in the recovery process. Those of us in the recovery world are not considering who we are in the matter of substance use disorder; we are building an environment of helplessness by enabling belief systems that sabotage choice.

The possibility of the extraordinary for Chris, his family, and the facilitators of his treatment cannot exist as a future reality while everyone is operating from behaviors defined by their past pain and trauma. Trapped in a context that cannot fathom possibility, we are managing addiction instead of developing the capacity to create our lives consciously. As long as we continue to place our pain into the future and blame others for our results, we will never be able to explore what is truly possible. The insights that create space for an extraordinary future exist out of examining what drives fear-based decision-making and enables the lack of self-awareness that keeps us enslaved to our ego.

The ego is a popular concept, but the ego itself is elusive and difficult to distinguish. To distinguish is to see the difference between two things, like the color red from blue. The distinction between these colors is clear: we can see the color red and the color blue even if we do not know the names of the colors like a one-year-old child. A toddler is able to comprehend the difference and quickly make blue their favorite color. However, the ego is not clearly recognizable; it is within us: it hides in us, disguised as us. The ego's camouflage makes it almost impossible to examine because we cannot separate who we are from the ego. Furthermore, we examine the ego through a lens created by the ego, which adds to its elusive nature. Conscious creation will remain lost as long as we are unaware of how the ego operates.

As we learn how the ego operates, we empower ourselves to transform. We can develop the capacity to tear down the existing framework that enables the ego to control the direction of our lives. Disconnection and ignorance enable the ego to operate. While we may not realize it, the ego disconnects us from the people we love and takes control of our decision-making.

The ego finds its salvation in the position that it takes. Positions like "best practice" or "right action" generate the lens through which we view our reality, which in time, forms an identity: "I am right." The "I" is the identity, and the ego thrives in it. The ego hides its identity in a clever disguise, presenting its thoughts and feelings as our own. We are often fooled by the ego's disguise, which leaves us disconnected from others. Each time the ego establishes a position, we think it is protecting us, which is another reason why we buy into its thinking and believe our actions are "right." No matter what results the ego produces, we are trapped in a reality created by our ego. This is why people can be sober but remain depressed, anxious, and dead inside. It is why we cannot build healthy relationships, and our children duplicate our patterns. We are trapped in a reality generated by our reactions to our ego.

The ego urges us to believe that its identities are good for us. It has enrolled us in believing that changing ourselves for the "better" (like weight loss, colored contacts, or a new career) is the right thing to do. However, for "better" to exist, the ego must first devise a problem and a solution for that problem, which then motivates us to solve the problem. It must make our current experience wrong, bad, or not good enough. Now under the guise of getting "better," we do what the ego tells us to do, and we may be enjoying our new career! However, while we are under the control of the ego, "better" can only be derived from "worse." The ego does not know sweet without sour or good without bad. This means that we will always be in touch with our pain; as we strive to change for the "better," we imprison ourselves in a vicious cycle. No matter what we have, we will always want more. We can be sober, have our dream job, and have our family back together, but still be unhappy because we are unintentionally operating from a mechanism born out of our trauma. We are identifying with our pain instead of confronting it. The ego says, 'I am worthless,' and we believe it, denying ourselves the freedom to process our worthlessness and move on with our lives. The ego is born out of our trauma.

Our past pain is not our current reality, but the ego will have us believe that we are victims.

The ego does not have our best interests in mind. The ego only cares about its identity and what sustains that identity. Unless we develop self-awareness, we will continue to think our ego's thoughts and feel its feelings as though they are our own. What we believe to be our reality will be a manifestation of our past pain. Our past pain is not our current reality, but the ego will have us believe that we are victims. We will allow the ego to tell us what is real and what is not real, what is possible and what is not possible. We will unintentionally disconnect ourselves from the world so that the ego can remain in control.

In the same way that Chris cannot use drugs and alcohol and be in recovery, his family and facilitators cannot use the ego and be in recovery from the ego. We cannot overcome our struggle with the ego by feeding it the answers that it needs to survive. The ego's need for answers and rules to follow holds very little insight. As we continue to live our lives from the fear of being worse—an ego-generated identity—we are left in the same context that drove us to seek change. We will be sober and continue producing the same undesirable results. Like a hamster on a wheel, no matter how effective we are in turning the wheel, we are left with the same pain. Unless we learn how to consciously create our lives, we will continue to operate outside the realm of possibility, existing in an illusion that is held in place by the ego's identity, and our past pain will continue to become our future reality.

The good news is that the ego's identities do not have to determine our future. The ego's identities are illusions, and when we buy into them, we trap ourselves in a reality defined by our unresolved pain and trauma. The ego wants us to believe that our thoughts, feelings, and behaviors revolve around the notion that our problems are external and not internal. Blinded by our ego, we cannot see that our depressive states of being are generated out of our adherence to ego identities. Our ego will have us believe that our depression is genetic or circumstantial. Anxiety disorders are generated out of ways we interpret the future; we believe that we have no control over our lives. The illusionary reality generated by our ego sets relapse in motion through thoughts and feelings that make substance abuse the best solution to our problems. We believe that our life is out of control as we unintentionally generate a cycle of dysfunction. Marriages dissolve, and children experience absent parents glued to their cell phones. Emotionally immature people raise children in ways that facilitate a future of addiction.

As long as we believe that our life experience is happening to us rather than embracing the possibility that is generated by us, we will continue to align our life experience with ego-generated identities. We will continue to recreate pain by reacting to the ego's desires rather than accessing the freedom to be creative. There is no answer, directive, or action that can remove us from the ego's identities while the ego is directing our behavior. Rather, we must transform the role that our unresolved past trauma plays in generating our future environment and play a bigger game than what our ego believes is possible. We must play a game that the ego cannot control, leveraging the power of choice to create a life extraordinary and sober.

Playing a New Game

The creative act is transformative. Creativity exists out of making a commitment to playing a bigger game, which sets in motion the possibility of transcending the ego. When we play a game, our ego's competitive nature calls us to participate at our best. The ego wants to win. It wants to be acknowledged for being special and unique. We can exploit the ego's inherent drive to win and rise above it through our commitment to playing the game. As the player, we become fully connected to the present moment in the game, not the ego. Fear and doubt are left behind; the ego vanishes as the player accesses the present moment.

Life is a behavioral practice field that provides the opportunity to play to achieve our dreams. Rules, boundaries, and best practices give structure to the game. The ego thrives in this structure and plays to be right or wrong, win or lose. However, while playing to achieve our consciously designed future, what is beyond the grips of the ego, we must set aside the rules and the ego's need to perform correctly. We must even give up the need to win the game to access transcendence. We cannot come from the need to win or to be right and play at our best. As we explore the power of the creative act from our commitment to our transformation, our failures teach us how to play for something greater than ego gratification.

In his book *The Inner Game of Tennis*, W. Timothy Gallwey explains how we can transcend the ego to access peak performance. We all interact with our ego, and the nature of this interaction determines the quality of our lives. Gallwey identifies Self 1, the teller, and Self 2, the doer. In *Mind Dynamics's* approach, Self 1 is the ego, and Self 2 is the conscious, creative self. Gallwey writes, "Within each player, the kind of relationship that exists between Self 1 and Self 2 is the prime factor in determining one's ability to translate his knowledge of technique into effective action. In other words, the key to better tennis—or better anything—lies in improving the relationship between the conscious teller Self 1 and the natural capabilities of Self 2."

It is helpful to imagine Self 1, the ego, and Self 2, the conscious self, as different aspects of the same person to understand the relationship between the two of them: "'Ok, dammit, keep your stupid wrist firm,' he orders. Then as ball after ball comes over the net, Self 1 reminds Self 2, 'Keep it firm. Keep it firm. Keep it firm.' Monotonous? Think how Self 2 must feel! It seems as though Self 1 thinks Self 2 does not hear well or has a short memory, or is stupid." The ego thinks that it is right all the time; it must make the conscious creative self dysfunctional and wrong in order to stay in control of our behavior.

Notice how the ego sabotages the player's ability to be effective; this is the same framework in which we generate our lives when we are not aware of how the ego works. Gallwey continues, "...reflect on the state of mind of a player who is said to be 'hot' or 'playing in the zone.' Is he thinking about how he should hit each shot? Is he thinking at all? Listen to the phrases commonly used to describe a player at his best: 'He's out of his mind'; 'He's playing over his head'; 'He's unconscious'; 'He doesn't know what he's doing.'" The common factor in each of these descriptions is that some part of the mind is not active. Athletes in most sports use similar phrases, and the best of them know that their peak performance never comes when they're thinking about it." The player who transcends Self 1 is able to access what is truly possible for human beings by transforming their relationship to their ego. The player is no longer playing from the framework created by the ego, but rather playing for the transcendence of the ego's identities. The directions by Self 1 are not the issue: our ego and its identities will always be with us. Dysfunction arises when we allow our ego to dictate our behavior and we construct our lives based on our reactions to its identities.

What is currently seen as a choice is actually fear-based decision-making that enables the ego to duplicate past pain as our future reality.

We have the opportunity to explore why we do not trust ourselves, why we do not examine where our thoughts and feelings come from, and why we do not shift from our current results to the results that we desire. As we explore the quality of our lives before, during, and after sobriety, we can begin to see that most people have very little access to choice. What is currently seen as a choice is actually fear-based decision-making that enables the ego to duplicate past pain as our future reality. Decisions close us off to possibility: we are actually murdering all other options. The word *decide* employs *-cide*, like suicide, the murder of oneself; homicide, the murder of someone else; and regicide, the murder of a king. The word *choice* is creative: we are selecting from possibility. The current landscape of recovery operates from the ego's positions, enforcing rules and right practices that may save people's lives, but people are trapped inside an environment that enables feelings of emptiness that drive relapse and death. *Mind Dynamics* invites the recovery world to embrace the possibility of creating an environment that facilitates the transcendence of the ego's identities and empowers people to choose life extraordinary and sober.

Prepare for a New Future

Mind Dynamics is committed to teaching individuals, families, and the recovery community how to create an environment that facilitates long-term sobriety by embracing their capacity to choose life extraordinary and sober. The extraordinary exists out of transcending ego identities, creating connections with friends and family members, overcoming depression and anxiety, improving health, and achieving peak performance in the workplace.

Like the game of tennis, there are rules and structure to the recovery process. 12-Steps, cognitive behavioral therapy, and community therapy have proven to be effective in establishing sobriety; *Mind Dynamics* is not trying to change the rules of the game. We are inviting people to play the game of recovery for the transformation of oneself rather than establishing sobriety while sabotaging choice. Our goal is *not* to make people "get better." "Getting better" is a position devised by the ego to enable the ego's existence; it identifies substance use disorder as a sickness, which places that sickness into our future.

Consider where following the ego has taken us: sobriety while sabotaging choice.

There is a difference between playing a game by the rules and playing for transcendence. To play a game, a player must observe the rules; otherwise, the player is not able to join the game. However, to access peak performance in the game, the player must choose to transcend the rules of the game. If a person plays from the awareness of merely following the rules, the player loses access to peak performance and will inevitably produce poor results. The player will be focused on playing right rather than performing. If we play merely to follow the rules of recovery, we allow the ego to take control over our behavior, and we will produce results limited by the ego's identities. This is why a person can be sober but generate the same results that they had before they chose sobriety, including dysfunctional relationships, feelings of deadness, depression, anxiety, and relapse.

Consider where following the ego has taken us: *sobriety while sabotaging choice*. We cannot produce different results in the future unless we change our current behavior by confronting our ego and its identities. Because of its desire to remain in control of our lives, our ego will not allow us to imagine a world without substance use disorder. However, as we rise above the rules of the game, we gain access to the world of possibility, and this is how we access life extraordinary and sober.

Chapter 2: Family Environment

CONVENTIONAL TREATMENT INVOLVES FAMILIES in the recovery process. However, families and people who choose sobriety are commonly approached separately: families (who are not seen as the problem) are invited to help manage their loved one's (who are seen as the problem) substance use disorder. The person who chooses recovery is approached as someone who is sick, and that sickness lives in their future. *Mind Dynamics* focuses on bringing healing to both families and people struggling with substance use disorder. In our continuum of care, *Life Extraordinary Approach Process* (LEAP), families learn how to create an inspiring environment that empowers the entire family to succeed in the face of adversity. Families learn how to identify and work through unresolved pain, repressed fears, and resentments to access the freedom to succeed and fail in life. Families discover the experience of a nurturing environment and learn how to facilitate the type of environment that creates love and connection rather than living into a future created out of past trauma.

> As we explore our ability to choose and the decisions we make, we can either let our ego generate our environment or learn to create the quality of our lives consciously.

The two primary positions that transform families are choice and environment. The genesis of recovery is the choice to be sober. Environment is the space that holds choice and drives behaviors. When a family creates an environment out of their unresolved past pain, that family dynamic will enable substance abuse, relapse, and death. Families can access life extraordinary and sober through the journey of self-discovery. As we explore our ability to choose and the decisions we make, we can either let our ego generate our environment or learn to create the quality of our lives consciously. The environment that we create determines what is possible for our family now and in the future.

Creating a New Environment

A continuum of care must evolve with the recovery process, which introduces new challenges in each stage of recovery. We have noticed that people who choose abstinence are often left without the necessary long-term skills to succeed in life, sometimes even after completing a rigorous 12-Step process. The recovery world is effective at establishing sobriety and the beginning stages of recovery but offers little support with the more complex life challenges as recovery evolves.

People who choose recovery will struggle as they face challenges such as:

- Now that I am sober, how do I love my children while managing healthy boundaries?
- How do I inspire my family to choose love and connection?
- How do I access a career that produces financial freedom?

Unfortunately, many people feel frustrated by the existing recovery options. The progressive nature of recovery necessitates an evolutionary continuum of care. The therapeutic process must evolve, matching the ever-changing internal and external landscapes of people in different stages of the recovery process.

Back in March 2021, I found myself at my lowest point. It had been 10 years since my deployment to Afghanistan and 7 years since I got sober. On the surface, I was a successful recovering addict and disabled combat vet with a degree and working my dream job as a therapist. But I felt dead inside. Stuck. I was still on methadone with no end date in sight. For more than 20 days a month, I suffered from migraines or migraine-related pain. I was isolated and alone. Scared and stuck. I had had enough and planned to kill myself by May 2022 if I was not "better." A week after making my suicide plan, I got a call from Pete Lotterhos and began my transformational work. Since that phone call, I have created a life I never believed possible. I am in my first healthy relationship in years; I started a new career where I am driven by my passion for others; I am no longer on methadone, I am a part of a strong community, and I have no migraines! I live with integrity by making and managing agreements, and I take responsibility for my life and my results. — Paul K.

Mind Dynamics argues that the environment that produces addiction is not interrupted by the traditional recovery process. If people who choose sobriety are returned to the same circumstances that produced addictive behaviors, those behaviors will live in the future. The environment must change. People must learn how to consciously create, step by step, an environment that establishes connection, renews relationships, and heals depression and anxiety. Such an environment empowers people to succeed in the face of adversity.

> **Our environment does not happen to us; it is generated by us.**

Families can learn how to create an inspirational environment that facilitates the extraordinary rather than simply managing addiction. The recovery world is very effective in its singular goal of establishing sobriety to keep people alive; however, it does not explore the creative act—the ability to dream and achieve. When such a possibility is overlooked, individuals and families are not taught how to create a functional and healthy environment that facilitates the type of connection that transforms the future of recovery.

Mind Dynamics introduces the insight that our circumstances do not dictate our environment. Our environment does not happen *to* us; it is generated *by* us. Our external environment is generated from our internal context, meaning how we think, feel, speak, and perceive builds our environment. Our internal way of being forms our external reality. The real work begins once we understand that we have always generated our environment. We have always been fully responsible for the quality of our lives, and that responsibility extends to families and their role in building an environment that inspires recovery.

> Families can learn how to create an environment that inspires their loved ones to choose life extraordinary and sober.

As we examine our lives, we will see that our external environment mirrors our internal context. By holding onto our trauma (our internal context), we will unintentionally duplicate that trauma as our future (our external environment). For example, the rejection that a person felt as a child may exist today in all of their relationships, which results in an inability to connect with others. This inability to connect interrupts one's ability to parent, be a supportive spouse, and perform in the workplace. Many people struggle to establish genuine connection with others as a way to protect themselves from confronting their past pain. By transforming our relationship to our past experiences, we introduce new possibilities to the context from which we think, feel, speak, and perceive. This new context of thought empowers us to create a new environment—a transformed future. Now, our choices are driven by possibility rather than fear, and our existing and future relationships are transformed. Families can learn how to create an environment that inspires their loved ones to choose life extraordinary and sober.

We all have the opportunity to learn how to create an environment that inspires possibility.

Mind Dynamics teaches families that our environment is created from context, and we know that the current environment needs to change in order to heal substance use disorder. The context that created the dysfunctional environment is generated by the ego, which forms its identities based on the things it has and the things that it does not have. We might have a car, but we may not like our car. We may have a place to live but feel upset that we cannot afford to buy a better house. Our ego uses our circumstances to diminish the quality of our lives. We allow our ego identities to give meaning to our experiences. Cars and houses hold no meaning in themselves. The lack of a car or house also holds no meaning. Until we build the capacity to choose, we will continue to use the ego's identities to construct the context from which we build our environment. We will make things right and wrong and play by the rules that allow the ego to thrive. As we explore ourselves and our responses to what we have and do not have, we will begin to see that we are living in a reality that we generated rather than a reality that is happening to us. We all have the opportunity to learn how to create an environment that inspires possibility.

The truth is this: our trauma does not need to play a role in the construction of our future environment.

We can generate our environment from a context that is defined by our ego or create an environment that is empowered by choice. Without developing self-awareness, we will generate our present reality out of our past pain. For example, if we assume that people will hurt, reject, and abandon us, we will behave in alignment with that expectation. This dysfunctional way of thinking and feeling can become the lens through which we see the world—authenticity is lost. Your reality is now made up; it has become make-believe; it is filtered through the lens created by your trauma, which is why our only option is to build internal barriers against connection with others. We have to leave before we are hurt. Our dysfunctional results are predetermined by our unwillingness to confront our unresolved trauma. We sabotage our future, our relationships, and our recovery by 'deciding' from a context that holds in place our past pain. The truth is this: our trauma does not need to play a role in the construction of our future environment.

The environment that produces addiction is the problem, not the person who chooses recovery.

We expand our capacity to choose by exploring how we bring meaning to our current life experience, our current reality. We can learn how to consciously create the quality of our lives by transforming the context from which we build our environment. Life is not happening to us; it is created by us!

Both families and their loved ones in recovery have the opportunity to learn how to create an environment that inspires health, wealth, and well-being. The environment that produces addiction is the problem, not the person who chooses recovery. From this perspective, we cannot blame the person in recovery for dysfunctional family relationships. The moment we begin to explore how we generate our environment, we can address what makes the most significant difference in people's lives: the individual's capacity to consciously create their life.

When families confront their emotional addiction, they will transform their future by shifting the context from which they build their environment.

Everyone in the family is responsible for the impact that their decisions have on the environment that sets in motion a future characterized by either addiction or recovery. Each individual in the family, not just the person who chooses recovery, has the opportunity to transform their environment by taking complete responsibility for the context in which they operate.

Mind Dynamics argues that unless people develop self-awareness, they are addicted to the emotions associated with their unresolved past pain and trauma. In her 2010 book *Molecules of Emotion*, Candace Pert demonstrated that our body becomes addicted to our emotional experiences in the same way that a person can develop a dependence on substances. Everyone in the family, not just the person who chooses recovery, is an addict who compulsively uses their emotions to create their lives. When families confront their emotional addiction, they will transform their future by shifting the context from which they build their environment.

Emotional Addiction

Mind Dynamics describes emotional addiction as a person's dependency on generating an environment that duplicates past pain. This dependency is chemical, and the addiction is literal. Emotional addiction carries with it a destructive cycle that causes us to sabotage our relationships and our personal and professional lives. *Mind Dynamics* invites the recovery community to commit to emotional sobriety and operate from self-awareness to avoid emotional relapse.

Emotional addiction is a function of an individual's ego identity ("I am inadequate") and the emotional components associated with that identity (how I feel about being inadequate). The emotions associated with emotional addiction are a cocktail of feelings that can include fear, anger, sadness, and regret. It is not a singular feeling like anxiety or depression but rather a grouping of feelings that enable our ego's identity, which then validates fear-based decision-making. Validation is when the ego tells us what is good and right; for example, it tells us that we are right about our decision to disconnect from the people we love by labeling the relationship "toxic." Unless we learn otherwise, this context of victimization will dominate our behavior, creating our future, and of course, we will feel unhappy with the results—it is our addiction. Emotional addiction, like any addiction, is compulsive and takes over our decision-making, leaving no room to choose behaviors that empower the extraordinary.

Our lives exist to validate the identity "I am inadequate" in the same way that an alcoholic's physiology is dependent on alcohol.

The "I" in the statement "I am inadequate" is driven by an addiction to emotional responses. The "I" has lost the ability to choose; there is only addictive behavior; nothing else matters or exists. We arrange our entire lives to validate the identity "I am inadequate" in the same way that an alcoholic's physiology is dependent on alcohol. Families are unable to take risks and manage boundaries for the same reason: they are validating their identity to access their physiological dependence on emotions like fear, anxiety, and anger. Their brains are wired to want to feed on and feel negative emotions, and the ego demands to be right about that addiction. This emotional addiction drives dysfunctional behaviors and substance abuse disorder. Mothers are enablers and fathers are emotionally unavailable because their emotional addiction determines their behavior. They are chemically addicted to their emotions in the same way that people who choose recovery from substance abuse are struggling with dependency. By committing to emotional sobriety, families can create an environment that drives long-term recovery. A continual development of self-awareness will prevent a return to emotional reactivity: emotional relapse.

Pain is our drug of choice, and we cannot see that we fight to feel our pain.

Mind Dynamics shows families how most people are unintentionally building their lives in a way that validates their emotional addiction. To fuel our emotional addiction, we build our reality utilizing our ego-generated identity, such as "I did not get the job," "I cannot create a marriage that works," or "I do not have a car as nice as the neighbor's." Pain is our drug of choice, and we cannot see that we fight to feel our pain. We think, feel, speak, and perceive in a way that enables our lives to revolve around our emotional addiction. This addiction actually began in childhood. For example, when our parents got divorced, we made their divorce our fault. We built identities to justify feeling our pain: "I am worthless" or "I am a victim." We begin building our identities early in life, and those identities will run our lives in adulthood. Our past dictates our future.

Emotional addiction drives dysfunction in our families. There are mothers in every city in the country that do all the household chores, take care of the children, and try to satisfy their husbands, all while working a full-time job. These mothers then complain about their needs not being met, but their behavior sets them up to feel the same pain that they felt as little girls when their parents got divorced. The amount of energy they exert in order to feel bad is unbelievable. We live our lives to feel what we are addicted to feeling and then complain about the quality of our lives.

Common complaints include:

- Worthlessness
- Inadequacy
- Shame
- Depression
- Anxiety
- Self-doubt
- Victimization
- Self-harm
- Rage
- Passivity
- Isolating
- Perfectionism
- Procrastination
- Controlling
- Dependency
- Codependence
- Enmeshment
- Enabling
- Overwhelmed
- Abusive
- Distrusting
- Disconnecting
- Irresponsible
- Lack of self-care
- Pretending
- Hiding

These complaints produce pain that drives emotional addiction, which is why we are always defending, deferring, hiding, lying, and commiserating with others over our problems. We generate dysfunctional behaviors out of our fear of rejection and avoid taking risks at work in order to feel our pain. All our complaints exist out of our unintentional commitment to feed our chemical dependence on our pain, which becomes the environment in which we raise our children.

Our Children and the Future

Our emotional addiction controls our choices and determines the environment that we build, which sabotages our children's

capacity to achieve. Our children are born into a pre-existing context that holds in place our trauma. Our pain is their playground. Their interaction with the world starts with our best intentions: "I am going to always be there for my children because my parents were not there for me. My parents didn't guide me, so I will guide my daughter; she has to go to college, work hard, and have all the things that I didn't have. I am not going to yell because I remember how it felt to be yelled at. I will give her whatever she wants because no one met my needs." However, as we avoid our true feelings and try to fix our past through our children, we enable all kinds of dysfunction to make up for our lack of nurturing, and our best intentions duplicate the same trauma that we were born into.

As we try to generate an environment that is the opposite of our childhood experiences, we unintentionally duplicate our trauma. This insight is difficult to hear; perhaps, it is even unsettling. Our decisions are predetermined and are not controlled by our conscious mind. Our best intentions are grounded in our past. We are still coming from our trauma as we form our idealistic goals. It is inevitable that we will duplicate our pain, and it's painful to see our children live out our addictive patterns. Trapped in our pain, we are blind to possibility.

The commitment for the mother in the example above to always be there for her daughter exists out of the belief that the mother was not cared for as a child, which generated an identity of worthlessness. She was committed to her daughter having what she did not have; however, this way of operating duplicates the same worthlessness in her daughter: overbearing parenting and enabling generates the same insecure child who doesn't trust herself to perform. For example, under the guise of "I will not tolerate your drama," we avoid, criticize, or reject, which breeds the drama we are seeking to avoid. The wounded child in us cannot build a nurturing environment because it has no access to choice.

A child who was raised in an abusive household with drug addiction and alcoholism can identify with rejection and abandonment, "I am worthless,"and never learn how to listen for acceptance. Families do not automatically know how to set boundaries that inspire the whole family to achieve. Children are not learning how to make choices that drive creative self-expression. The choices we make and the environment that we form is the future that we and the people we love live in—our future-created reality is our past.

The reluctance we have to accept who we are and who we are not, what we have and what we don't have, triggers our emotional addiction that duplicates our pain in our children. Acceptance is the only option. Our children are not ours. We do not own them. Perhaps we can say we "rent" them for a period of time, and soon they will be off on their own, duplicating the trauma they picked up from interacting with their parents. By removing our ideals and listening, we will see that within each of us and our children exists a vision that can be created. A vision that is grounded in the freedom to be expressive. Rather than trying to change other people, consider acceptance.

Chapter 3: A Transformed Future

THE FIRST STAGE OF RECOVERY addresses physical addiction and includes learning to abstain from drugs and alcohol. This stage is where traditional recovery is most effective. When people choose recovery, the first and most important step is to stop the destructive behavior that will save their lives: abstain from drugs and alcohol. The second stage is behavioral addiction, which includes abstinence from overworking, gambling, sexual compulsion, gaming, emotional eating, social media, shopping, relationships, exercise, dieting, and more. We have found that people will shift from chemical addiction to behavioral addiction. By abstaining from harmful chemicals and destructive behaviors, our clients gain access to stage three recovery. *Mind Dynamics's* outpatient facility addresses stages one and two of recovery using cognitive behavioral therapy and refers our clients to support groups like SMART Recovery or 12-Steps. In the third stage, there is a shift from the person choosing abstinence to a radical transformation of the entire community: we teach families how to overcome emotional addiction and create a new environment.

People in recovery and their families are living their lives in a dysfunctional context that generates an environment that enables their emotional addiction. *Mind Dynamics* places the person in recovery and the family on the same page by addressing each person's emotional addiction.

Each person in the family has the opportunity to explore their role in the family dynamic that enables addictive behavior.

By creating a level practice field for recovery, families can create an environment that inspires sobriety. The whole family can work towards the quality of care necessary to access and sustain long-term recovery. The self-aware family is able to take full responsibility for their role in the recovery process; there is no longer any room for blaming or criticizing the person with substance use disorder for the dysfunctional family environment. Each person in the family has the opportunity to explore their role in the family dynamic that enables addictive behavior. The moment the entire family chooses to work on themselves and their emotional compulsions, a conversation is born that has the power to transform their future. The conversation at the dinner table now sounds like "I" rather than "you." For example, "I now see that I…" rather than

"You need to stop…" The family is now operating in an environment that is empowering, inclusive, and healing rather than sabotaging, divisive, and enabling. The family's environment transforms the instant its members choose to do the work it takes to heal themselves and access a conversation that facilitates conscious creation.

Inspirational Language Transforms

Our inner life is shaped by language. We shape our reality from our conversations with ourselves and the people around us. Our background and experience give us vocabulary for these conversations. All our life experiences, including our level of education and economic status, are generated from our inner conversations.

It does not matter where we come from; the language that we use to define ourselves shapes our future.

It is no secret that people who create wealth have a different mindset from people who operate from financial scarcity. We cannot generate financial freedom while listening from scarcity. The sentences we form about ourselves sentence us either to a life imprisoned by fear or a life of authenticity. Fear generates addiction to both substances and emotions, while aliveness inspires recovery, financial freedom, and fulfilling relationships. The way that people talk to themselves and experience the world before and after sobriety creates a future shaped by an inner conversation. It does not matter where we come from; the language that we use to define ourselves shapes our future. The words we speak to ourselves utilizes language that we can change.

Mind Dynamics teaches families how to use linguistic tools to drive a transformed future. We have seen above how the ego uses language to build its identity in the statement, "I am worthless." The ego uses language to establish that we are victims, "I am never good enough." However, we can take responsibility for our choices using a new approach: "I am responsible for generating an environment in order to feel my pain." Families have the power to transform their emotional addiction to build an environment that drives recovery. Our linguistic tools give our clients the vocabulary to confront the ego's identities to recognize emotional compulsions to set in motion new behaviors that bring about a future characterized by possibility. As families move through our curriculum, they learn how to use language to build an environment that inspires healing.

The ego cannot build an identity while we are choosing to be accountable.

Transformation begins with our ability to be fully accountable to ourselves and others for the environment that we generate. The ego cannot build an identity while we are choosing to be accountable. When we operate from a commitment to being fully accountable for our behaviors, there is no room for the ego to use language to say, "I am worthless," make us feel bad about being worthless, and drive us to generate a reality that facilitates worthlessness. Accountability is one's capacity to take responsibility for their results. Accountability cannot function partially; it can only exist completely. We are fully responsible for the results that we generate or create in our lives; there is no gray area. In order to transform our lives, we must learn how to take full responsibility for the creative act of our lives and the impact that we have on others.

Absolute Accountability

Accountability is a choice that drives behaviors that transform our relationship with the ego. The conversation that creates absolute accountability exists in one's willingness to take full responsibility for their thinking, feeling, speaking, and perceiving and the impact that their decisions have on others. Instead of surrendering to the ego's identity, "I am worthless," we can use language to generate possibility, "I now see that I created an environment that enabled me to feel like a victim." Notice that both statements employ "I," but one is an ego identity, and the other is a statement of self-awareness that destroys the ego's capacity to dictate our behavior. The moment we take responsibility for the impact of our decisions, the blindness produced by the ego is removed, and we are able to see how we generate our results. Blaming is no longer an option. The need to disconnect from others vanishes, and what arises is the opportunity to create consciously. When families learn how to integrate absolute accountability into their lives, they gain access to language that empowers them to successfully navigate the hurdles of the recovery process.

> *Through the training I received, I got to see my game of needing to be liked and how that game has caused me to play small in my life. I got the opportunity to see the power in taking responsibility as opposed to blaming others and trying to change them. Since I received the training through Mind Dynamics, I cannot unsee what I've seen. If I choose to avoid responsibility, that's on me and nobody else. I have the power to choose and create my life using 100% accountability. I am now a top performer in my company and in a job role that I used to watch other people do and resent them for it. I have created boundaries and externalized my truth to those in my life and have been able to create meaningful and intentional relationships. As I've taken responsibility for my insecurities of needing to be liked and gone about life in a way that may put*

my need at risk, I have created much greater oppor-
tunities and experiences that have given me a life
greater than I could've imagined before Mind Dy-
namics. – Carly A.

There are three stages of accountability: self, other, and other to other. First, we develop our ability to be accountable by choosing to be responsible for what we generate in our own lives based on the way we think, feel, speak, and perceive. We must realize that our circumstances did not shape our environment or generate our results. We are responsible for the inner conversation that produced our external circumstances. We have the opportunity to take responsibility for the way we interpret the language of others. It does not matter what someone else says; we give meaning to what they say and use that meaning to generate our emotional responses.

Then, in stage two of accountability, other, we have the opportunity to own the way that other people see and hear us. Our tone, language, body language, and even our clothing generate an environment that impacts others and their life experiences. Stage two invites us to interact with others in such a way that they are inspired to create desirable results. In the same way that we give meaning to the language and actions of others, other people give meaning to the things that we say and do.

We are responsible for the results that other people are producing.

Stage three of accountability, other to other, explores the impact that we have on others as they create their lives. Stage three of accountability explains how the manager is responsible for the results of their team, shows that parents are accountable for the success of their children, and explores how the recovery world has the ability to create life extraordinary and sober. We are responsible for the results that other people are producing. Stage three of accountability does not propose that we have control over other people's actions. The illusion that we can control others is created by the ego to keep us from being fully accountable.

The three stages of accountability produce self-awareness that transforms the quality of our lives. Most of us do not have the self-awareness needed to understand how we are creating our environment, making choices, and generating results. Most of us blame others and make them responsible for our personal experiences. In doing so, we blind ourselves to our role in creating our lives. When we focus on our role in generating our lives, we access self-awareness and create access to possibility. As we explore the impact that we have on the people we love, the same insight applies. We get to see how we enable them to create poor results. We have the opportunity to take responsibility for the environment that we create and the impact that it has on other people's capacity to consciously create their lives. With respect to recovery, we can see that we generated the environment that produced addiction, and we can learn how to choose what inspires healing.

By taking responsibility for something that seems outside of our control, the results that other people produce, we have access to two insights. One, the impact that we have on how other people create their lives, and two, what it takes to create a new reality. Absolute accountability empowers us to see past the veil produced by the ego that keeps us disconnected. The ego finds its identity in the language, "I am the victim," "I have no control," and "I cannot do anything about it." These identities trigger our emotional addiction, render us helpless, and cut us off from creating new realms of possibility with the people we love. We walk blindly into the future until we develop the type of self-awareness required to see how we generate our current reality and the impact that we have on the choices of others.

The moment we see how we generate what exists in our lives, we can create new behavior that produces new results.

Self-awareness is the key to transforming our future. Families can use language that drives transformation, such as: "I understand that I am completely responsible for generating the environment that sabotaged your recovery by not establishing healthy boundaries with you and tolerating an abusive relationship with your father. I am sorry that I was unable to see my role in generating your relapse. This is a learning experience for me." This new conversation creates space for a supportive connection in which blame cannot exist. There is no room for language that enables the ego to generate identities like, "You should stop using heroin," "You should not speak to me that way," "You need to get a job," and "You have to learn how to be an adult." Out of making the difficult commitment to being fully accountable, we transform the conversation from criticism to acceptance: "I understand that life after sobriety is scary, and out of my commitment to you and your life, let's explore what inspires you rather than what merely keeps you alive. Are you willing to explore new possibilities with me?"

Healing becomes possible for everyone in the family who is willing to play a bigger game than sobriety; each individual must establish a commitment to their personal transformation. The moment we see how we generate what exists in our lives, we can create new behavior that produces new results. Old behaviors that produce addiction and hinder recovery can be replaced by new behaviors that create possibility for new, inspiring results.

Transparency and Radical Honesty

Mind Dynamics describes the language of accountability as transparency and radical honesty, which are the tools that bring about a new future. Language is the resource that human beings use to create their lives. Our language created our past, and language has the power to transform our future. Transparency is a conversation that exposes limitations rather than hiding them. Transparency includes clearly communicating one's feelings. We have the opportunity to authentically and fully feel our feelings. The ego encourages us to hide our emotional addiction to act like we are in control of our behavior. However, by choosing vulnerability over inauthenticity, we choose exposure rather than ego gratification. The choice to be transparent confronts the ego's impulse to look good, feel good, and be good, which disconnects us from peak performance and the people we love. The practice of transparency empowers us to see when we are generating an environment that enables us to feel our past pain in our personal and professional lives.

Radical honesty interrupts how the ego works in our lives. By choosing radical honesty, we are choosing to share the thinking, feeling, and perceiving that we have about ourselves and others that are normally repressed. On the other hand, if we avoid bringing to light things that make us and others look and feel bad, we trap ourselves and others in a dysfunctional environment by refusing to share our thoughts and confronting our feelings. If we cannot identify the breakdown, we cannot address it in a way that creates change. We can learn how to externalize the language of our internal dialogue in a way that transforms our relationship with our ego and brings out new realms of possibility for ourselves and others. We normally avoid discussing our anger, resentment, and insecurities with others because it is outside of our comfort zone, which then sets in motion a determined future. Our ego tells us that such conversations are sometimes cruel, which is why radical honesty is so important. Through language, we learn how to transform.

The key to radical honesty and transparency is learning how to create the space to be heard. While repression and denial create depression, anxiety, and disconnection that sabotage a person's power to create, transformative language heals. Learning how to integrate transparency, radical honesty, and accountability into family interactions builds a functional environment that defeats emotional addiction. Conversations that the family would normally avoid are now openly discussed because the family now has the emotional capacity to feel and discuss their feelings. Emotions that were avoided are now felt and shared. There is no longer a need for defense mechanisms that we previously used to hide our negative feelings. The environment in which the family operates is transformed through a commitment to accountability and a shift in language. Their future is now open to new worlds of possibility that the family previously did not have access to: life is a new adventure.

Emotional Integrity

The principle of emotional integrity builds on our capacity for absolute accountability, transparency, and radical honesty. Integrity is key to the success of sobriety and personal transformation. Integrity is not used to make a person right or wrong; it is the mechanism we use to acknowledge the results of our agreements. The ego holds integrity as a moralistic position to perpetuate identities such as "I am good if I have integrity" and "I am bad when I lack integrity."

Like accountability, integrity is absolute. We either have integrity or we do not; integrity is a total commitment. We are either "in" integrity, or we are "out" of integrity, and this is not good or bad. Integrity is not a moralistic position; there is no moralistic relationship with our results to make our results good or bad. Most people understand integrity as the alignment of our actions with what we say we are going to do and then see their results as good or bad. *Mind Dynamics* defines emotional integrity as a completely neutral state of being that gives us space to fully accept our emotions and take responsibility for the results that we generate. *Mind Dynamics's* approach to integrity includes fully feeling our feelings and understanding how those feelings impact our choices and the choices of others. We can choose to align our feelings with absolute accountability, transparency, and radical honesty because we no longer allow those feelings to determine our future. Our results are our results; they do not need to be tools that the ego uses to generate affirmation or shame.

It is important to understand how integrity works in the recovery process. People in recovery can learn how to be in integrity with their sobriety by fully experiencing any negative feelings associated with addiction. For example, many people who choose recovery will feel shame, which is a feeling that drives relapse when we experience it from a moralistic position, "I am ashamed of my addiction." The ego wants us to feel wrong about our shame, but the principle of emotional integrity invites us to feel our shame completely and use it to create a new reality.

> **When families have the self-awareness to separate what happened from the interpretation of what happened, they are empowered to create a new future.**

Mind Dynamics teaches individuals and families how to remove the moralistic position from integrity by distinguishing what happened from the interpretation associated with what happened. What happened is addiction; interpretation generates shame associated with addiction. By removing the moralistic position "I am bad" from "I am sick," the person is able to accept being sick without shame. Everyone is able to feel their feelings completely, and the door to peak performance opens. Families have the opportunity to transcend what is right and wrong, the rules of the game, and play for recovery.

We negate the ego's programmatic responses by learning how to separate what happened from our interpretation of what happened. What happened was the ball did not go in the hoop. This doesn't mean that we are a failure: that is an interpretation of what happened. What happened is someone spoke; our interpretation is that they insulted us. The car drove in front of us; it did not cut us off. Failure never happened, rejection never happened, abandonment never happened: they are all interpretations. We assigned pain to circumstance. When families have the self-awareness to separate what happened from the interpretation of what happened, they are empowered to create a new future.

Families can use the principle of emotional integrity to avoid duplicating shame in the recovery process. Everyone in the family can choose to overcome their emotional addiction by feeling and externalizing all of the feelings associated with addiction to create an environment that facilitates healing. We must confront and resolve our feelings of worthlessness, emptiness, and dependence and leverage those feelings rather than duplicate them in our lives. We can learn from our results and commit to new behaviors instead of hiding, defending, and lying to avoid the shame of failure. The ego makes failure wrong, so we are unwilling to take risks that set in motion the possibility of failure. We end up playing small in life and feeling dead inside. However, failure is the first step in mastery. No one cares that Babe Ruth led the league in strikeouts! People only see his success. The freedom to experiment and fail leads to the freedom to experiment and achieve. Families in the recovery process must gain access to the freedom to take the risk to fully feel and communicate their emotions. A nurturing environment is born when everyone in the family is empowered to work through the trials of being human and learn how to achieve in the face of resistance.

By choosing absolute accountability, transparency, radical honesty, and emotional integrity, a new relationship with the self is created that has the power to transform family dynamics from criticism to acceptance. As family members learn how to make choices in the face of resistance, engage in feelings instead of avoiding, and account for their personal experiences rather than blaming others, a nurturing environment is created. This environment creates the type of connection that invites nonjudgmental interactions that inspire people to choose life extraordinary and sober. Through practicing the behaviors that bring emotional endurance into our lives, the limiting self is confronted, and the person becomes empowered to access new behaviors and the capacity to achieve in the face of resistance. What was once perceived as a problem is now approached as possibility; a new relationship to adversity is created. The entire family is transformed.

A New Future

Mind Dynamics delivers a continuum of care that evolves with the ever-changing landscape of human development from initial sobriety to life extraordinary and sober.

I was introduced to Mind Dynamics after five years of sobriety. I was depressed, lost, and stagnant. I had absolutely no lust for life. Through doing the work with Mind Dynamics this past year, I no longer feel depressed. I have experienced connection with others that I did not think was possible. I now see that I have chosen my reality and that it is my responsibility for how I show up for the people in my life. This work has saved my friendships, given me new ones, and significantly strengthened all of my relationships. It is a beautiful feeling to be acknowledged by the people I love who see a difference in me and are inspired by the work I am doing! – Katherine M.

Both people who choose recovery and their families operate in an environment that drives addiction and relapse. *Mind Dynamics* teaches people how to develop the level of self-awareness required to transform the environment that is producing dysfunctional results. We inspire families to create the extraordinary by utilizing the language of absolute accountability, emotional integrity, transparency, and radical honesty.

Chapter 4: A New Sober Community

As THE EVER-CHANGING LANDSCAPE OF RECOVERY EVOLVES, the person in recovery and their family will come face to face with their ability to create together. *Mind Dynamics* takes a stand for life extraordinary and sober, which creates space for families to thrive in the face of resistance. We are committed to educating those in recovery, along with their families and peers, on how to transform the future by utilizing conventional treatments, engaging in sober living, and building a sober community.

Conscious creation exists out of making a commitment to take on and transform ego-driven operations. This new possibility begins when all participants in the recovery process are energized by the practice of absolute accountability, transparency, radical honesty, and emotional integrity. These core principles, when held in place by a community, create a behavioral practice field in which participants can build the emotional capacity necessary to transform past pain and trauma into life extraordinary and sober.

A *Mind Dynamics* Sober Community is a dynamic collection of individuals mutually encouraging and inspiring each other in the creative act of life-conscious creation. The formation of this community is grounded in the training of facility staff, families, and peers on how to build an environment that inspires success and views failure as an opportunity for growth. *Mind Dynamics* uses the educational program LEAP to teach families, peers, and those who have achieved sobriety how to integrate the creative process into long-term recovery.

Each individual has come to see that they are creating their lives—life is not happening to them.

A *Mind Dynamics's* Sober Community is built on a transformational process that is understood by first experiencing it, and then participants can learn how to give it away to others. Each member of the community—licensed facilitators, group leaders, persons choosing recovery, families, and peers—experience a way of thinking, feeling, speaking, and perceiving that is aligned with possibility. Our sober community is created by people who have experienced the extraordinary in their lives and are committed to creating space for others. This community is an extraordinary practice field for applying absolute accountability, transparency, radical honesty, and emotional integrity. Each individual has come to see that they are creating their lives—life is not happening to them.

A *Mind Dynamics* Sober Community provides the space for people to fully experience and reframe repressed feelings, which are rooted in childhood trauma and sabotage current performance. This process allows participants to create a new relationship with the thoughts and feelings associated with risk (good/bad, right/wrong, success/failure, and acceptance/rejection), and access the freedom to fully engage in life. While failures are inevitable when playing beyond our existing capacity, the nurturing environment of a *Mind Dynamics* Sober Community allows a shift in thinking. This reframing inspires breakthroughs into new realms of conscious creation. Adversity becomes an inspiration for transformation rather than a vehicle for shame.

Mind Dynamics engages in a new conversation about substance use and mental health disorders. The conversation changes from sobriety as the outcome of treatment to the first step in the creation of an inspiring life. In time, the establishment of sobriety becomes secondary to the creation of an environment that drives peak performance. Long-term sobriety and life extraordinary begin when those who choose sobriety and those who support their journey embrace possibility and believe that each person has the power to create their life consciously. *Mind Dynamics*'s mission is to reshape the future of recovery by establishing the type of sober community that fosters the transformation of oneself, creating an infectious aliveness that drives personal achievement, love, and acceptance.

The Breakdown

Facilities and those who choose sobriety, along with their family and peers, are currently operating in a dysfunctional environment that drives relapse and death when their continuum of care does not evolve to match their personal needs. For example, the primary focus in recovery is on saving lives, not producing life extraordinary. This breakdown sets up the possibility of overlooking additional diagnoses, emotional immaturity, and limited life skill development. Saving lives is clearly an important objective; we do not get to create the extraordinary if we are not alive. However, when sobriety is our singular focus, we miss addressing the person's capacity to consciously create their lives, which in the long run can sabotage one's commitment to their recovery.

It is common knowledge that substance abuse disorder often occurs in comorbidity with other mental health disorders. Here in Connecticut, the Department of Mental Health and Addiction Services (DMHAS) reports that 33% of their admissions had both substance use and serious mental health disorder (i.e., bipolar disorder, major depressive disorder, schizophrenia, and schizoaffective disorder) in 2021. In our research on the towns within 15 miles of our location, we found that DMHAS reported that only 12% of admissions had co-occurring substance use and serious mental health disorder. No numbers were presented for all the other mental health disorders as they occur with substance use disorder. The 2021 National Survey on Drug Use and Health reported similar low percentages.

The existing treatment that surrounds substance use disorder is not driving the type of environment that empowers aliveness in the face of adversity but rather enables deadness. Substance use disorder treatment facilities are more concerned with treating serious co-occurring mental health disorders with a high morbidity rate and are less focused on the long-term management of additional disorders like depression, anxiety, and ADD/ADHD after sobriety is achieved. This treatment approach is why so many people are sober but feel dead inside: their mental health is not diagnosed and treated in a way that alters the future. If someone with substance use disorder is diagnosed with a mental health disorder, the diagnosis is as a life sentence, which means it is managed indefinitely with medication. Effective treatments such as intensive individual and group therapy or cathartic emotional weekend workshops—if they are offered at all—are often led by facilitators who are unable to generate a transformative interaction, leaving patients and their families lacking the emotional skill set to live life extraordinary and sober.

Families, peers, and even therapists can be trapped in survival mode by monitoring sobriety and managing mental health disorders. As a result, treatment is not progressing as the client transitions through the recovery process. *Mind Dynamics* offers a continuum of care for clients and families who are ready to transition from broken to unbreakable. Our objective is to match the client's personal transformation with their recovery journey. Then, through our educational process, our clients transition from the choice to be sober to conscious creation. This includes individual, group, and community work. Every individual in the family (not singularly focused on the person who chooses sobriety) has the opportunity to build the emotional capacity and skills necessary to succeed in the real world: absolute accountability, radical honesty, transparency, and emotional integrity. The environment that drives healing is directly connected to the individual's capacity to consciously create the extraordinary.

Mind Dynamics uses the Adverse Childhood Experience Questionnaire (ACE) to help families see their trauma and invite them to participate in a no-cost group meeting with graduates of LEAP. In that meeting, our LEAP graduates share their ACE score and their transformative results. We focus on sharing, feeling, and accounting for trauma and the results of accessing sobriety and conscious creation. LEAP graduates have learned to leverage their sickness and have created the opportunity to thrive. The meeting sets in motion a conversation where being sick and extraordinary come to life. Graduates are acknowledged for their achievements, and new participants gain access to seeing what is possible for themselves and their families.

Most of us are convinced that life is happening to us. For example, we think that depression or anxiety is happening to us and that we have no control over our life experiences. In this victim context, focusing on survival is the only option. Confronting our feelings can be scary, painful, and unsettling. It can also be exciting, rewarding, and inspiring. Our outpatient programs, family therapy, and LEAP courses are designed to coach people on how to shift from identifying as victims to practicing absolute accountability. Once we see how the ego-created identities operate from our past pain, we can identify the inner struggles that generate dysfunction and create new behaviors that produce health, financial freedom, and long-term recovery.

It is easier to accept a diagnosis, avoid feelings, or manage emotional responses than it is to learn how to enjoy the experience of failure and rejection.

We all have the opportunity to gain access to the world of possibility for ourselves and others. Addiction cannot stop the creative act. Human beings generate the environment in which they live their lives. We determine the quality of our relationships, financial health, and self-care. We create the opportunity to confront the issues within ourselves and others. Additionally, we will not live life without intensely feeling the emotional responses associated with the decisions we make, as much as we may want to hide and numb ourselves. We cannot. We all have powerful feelings. Our emotional experiences include feelings of success and failure, acceptance and rejection, and deadness and aliveness. It is easier to accept a diagnosis, avoid feelings, or manage emotional responses than it is to learn how to enjoy the experience of failure and rejection.

A Performance-Oriented Environment

The genesis of performance is integrity. Integrity means keeping our word, and our word creates the quality of our life. In the context of recovery, our word can create sobriety and a new life that is filled with possibility. One's word sets in motion what becomes possible—a created future.

The recovery community is currently participating in a conversation that limits what is possible by singularly focusing on resources that drive sobriety. This conversation centers on identifying problems and then presenting solutions for those problems. This is how the ego operates. We use our conversations to exercise power and control over others and generate shame, guilt, and pain that reflects our past trauma. The recovery world has built a conversation that is characterized by scarcity of treatment and management of diseases. Substance use treatment facilities are filled with staff who are overwhelmed by the stress of treating disease, but only a tiny percentage of people with substance use disorder receive treatment for it, and almost no one with the disease feels that they need treatment. It is easy to feel that healing is scarce. Facilities and families are listening for and speaking about defeat and hopelessness rather than possibility. In reality, the disease creates access to the extraordinary. We can learn how to set in motion a conversation that brings to life the capacity for people to be sick and extraordinary. This new conversation creates space for people who hide to choose what is truly possible.

Mind Dynamics works with families to transform addiction, depression, and anxiety into peak performance by teaching people how to leverage integrity to drive purpose, passion, and mastery. We teach participants how to align personal and professional goals with long-term recovery. The practice of integrity is keeping your word when you make an agreement; this practice drives out all ambiguity in interactions with others, allowing for a multifaceted focus on sobriety and performance. Once the value for agreements is established and not seen as a vehicle for shame, guilt, or rejection, a new conversation is created that opens space for new results. Our training has a very clear target: the empowerment of the person's capacity to create their future consciously.

Addiction and sobriety both introduce possibility.

Each agreement sets in motion the opportunity to acknowledge breakthrough results and address the breakdown that sabotaged performance. Breakthrough and breakdown both create the opportunity to drive increased performance when held as possibility. Addiction and sobriety both introduce possibility.

The feeling of being overwhelmed is a common complaint. This feeling comes from and perpetuates disconnection both personally and professionally. A common reaction to overwhelm is hiding our true selves from the people we love, which enables resentment, relapse, and death. However, the complaint of feeling overwhelmed unveils new realms of possibility when we explore it through the perspective of absolute accountability. We can take total responsibility for our results by examining the origins of our feelings (our history), what we get out of our feelings (the payoff), and the truth about our feelings (ulterior motive). Then, we can set in motion the type of insight that creates space for new behavior. We have already examined how we generate a dysfunctional environment as a reaction to our past pain, our history. The payoff for feeling overwhelmed may be sleep, lying, or hiding. We may believe that we cannot handle our feelings anymore, making disconnection with others our only option. Absolute accountability empowers us to confront our ulterior motive: the truth is we are hiding from authentically feeling our feelings. Our decision to avoid confronting our feelings is rationalized by the belief that hiding is our best option; it is better to avoid than to feel anger, hurt someone else's feelings, or deal with someone else's anger.

When a community develops the capacity to view a problem as possibility, breakdowns become extraordinary opportunities for breakthrough performance.

By exploring the feeling of being overwhelmed through the lens of absolute accountability, our history, the payoff, and our ulterior motive are unveiled. The breakdown is now part of a conversation that holds the potential for insight and new behavior—personal transformation. The egoistic behaviors of avoiding emotional connection and personal responsibility come to the forefront. Now, a conversation can be created that produces new behaviors that transform our future. By exploring absolute accountability, not in a way to make the person feel wrong or bad, but rather as a way to access new behavior, a new future is created. When a community develops the capacity to view a problem as a possibility, breakdowns become extraordinary opportunities for breakthrough performance.

The inability for families to access possibility is evidence of the lack of support families receive when their loved ones choose sobriety. Effective communication gives us access to what will produce new behavior in our lives. Anything seen as a failure can be confronted and converted into inspiration when we are educated to view it from the perspective of possibility. When people fail, they often blame others, which rationalizes dysfunctional behavior and repression and avoids absolute accountability. By choosing to participate in a community that is committed to sobriety and performance, the individual and family can become emotionally available, inspired, and impeccable with themselves, the people they love, and the people in their community.

Without self-awareness, we have a limited vision of what is possible, our lack of integrity dictates our behavior, and we lose access to the insights that inspire new behaviors. However, individuals and families can learn how to envision the extraordinary and make and manage agreements in a way that drives results. Families can develop their capacity to create their lives in a sober community that is committed to performance.

Family members that have experienced the extraordinary have the emotional capacity to inspire the creation of a new environment that drives a transformed future.

The process of learning how to transform our future in the context of a sober community exists out of our commitment to healing our past pain, accepting ourselves and others, and envisioning what is truly possible with the people we love. The

Mind Dynamics Sober Community focuses on the transform-ative model of communication, which is grounded in the prin-ciple of absolute accountability. When families come from the position of being absolutely accountable for creating an envi-ronment that drives long-term recovery and full self-expres-sion, the person who chooses recovery can only be approached from the perspective of possibility. Families now have the abil-ity to view their loved one who chooses recovery as someone who is developing the capacity to choose the extraordinary, not merely as a person who will need a lifetime of medication and therapy to manage illness. This means that families have learned how to cultivate a conversation that inspires their loved ones to choose sobriety and embrace a passion for life. Family members that have experienced the extraordinary have the emotional capacity to inspire the creation of a new envi-ronment that drives a transformed future.

Mind Dynamics educates those in recovery, facilitators of recovery, families, and peers to confront personally imposed barriers to performance to create an environment that facili-tates the ability to thrive in the face of adversity. The develop-ment of emotional resilience is painful and empowers us to enjoy the experience of conscious creation; transforming our capacity to dream and achieve brings to existence the ability to live a designed life. Facilities, families, and peers must un-derstand that such a transformation is possible, and they have an obligation to inspire those who choose recovery to leverage pain to achieve peak performance. People who succeed have learned optimism: failure generates the capacity to achieve.

Empowered Peer-to-Peer Interactions

Those who choose recovery and achieve the extraordinary have a vital role in the *Mind Dynamics* Sober Community. For most *Mind Dynamics* clients, the journey begins with life-saving detox and our outpatient PHP/IOP/OP programs. Being healthy enough for personal transformation may also include medically assisted treatment, medications for mental health disorders, and family therapy. Once a person in recovery has achieved sobriety and received mental health treatment, that person may be healthy enough to develop their capacity to create a new life. The work of personal transformation is built out of the desire to thrive rather than simply manage disease, which is why we support our clients in discovering their next step. We match our client's level of care; step-by-step, we guide our clients from being sick to extraordinary.

Life Extraordinary Approach Process (LEAP), our educational continuum of care, is a training curriculum that inspires those in long-term recovery to develop the physical, mental, financial, and spiritual health needed to succeed. Graduates of LEAP are invited to form peer-to-peer relationships, lead groups, and large seminars. LEAP offers two educational paths for learning, our Life Skills Seminar Series and our Empowerment Training. Our Life Skills Seminar Series is divided into four categories: self-care, mental and emotional health, relationships, and financial management. Our Empowerment Training is deeper work consisting of three levels: Basic Training, Advanced Training, and the Advanced Training Empowerment Series.

Mind Dynamics trains peer-to-peer leaders to develop emotional resilience, engage in the conscious creation of their lives, and duplicate that possibility with others.

Mind Dynamics exists to teach individuals and families how to listen for and speak to possibility and access behaviors that inspire others. Peer-to-peer interactions are crucial in the conventional recovery process, but without developing their capacity to choose, most peers have access to sobriety but not life extraordinary. Many peers are sober but suffer from depression and anxiety and feel dead inside. In a *Mind Dynamics* Sober Community, peers who have achieved life extraordinary and sober inspire others to create sobriety and aliveness. *Mind Dynamics* trains peer-to-peer leaders to develop emotional availability, engage in the conscious creation of their lives, and inspire others to embrace the transformative power of choice. Peer-to-peer interactions include individual, group, and seminar settings that are educational in nature. Interaction between peers is a behavioral practice field. As peers practice creating space for others and learn how to work through their own personally imposed barriers to performance, healing occurs. Speaking the language of transformation, peer-to-peer interaction is characterized by absolute accountability, radical honesty, transparency, and emotional integrity. This community creates inspiring results.

The *Mind Dynamics* Sober Community empowers emotional endurance and personal mastery.

Peer-to-peer interactions will sometimes trigger memories of past trauma, but participants support each other in their transformation. Individual, group, and seminar work is held in place by peers who have succeeded in their personal transformation and are committed to driving breakthrough performance in themselves and others. The *Mind Dynamics* Sober Community empowers emotional endurance and personal mastery. Through practice, community members develop the ability to trust themselves and others. *Mind Dynamics's* objective is not only to teach people the skills to succeed, but to provide the time and space to achieve mastery. Mastery is created through time on task with an intensity comparable to competition. The disciplines of absolute accountability, radical honesty, transparency, and emotional integrity must be practiced with intensity and consistency to increase a person's capacity to perform under pressure. A *Mind Dynamics* Sober

Community is a performance-oriented environment that operates from the premise that each person can create their life and succeed in the face of great resistance.

Life Skills Seminar Series

We can discover our capacity to heal and achieve peak performance when we leverage our setbacks to access possibility. In our Life Skills Seminar Series, participants are invited to acknowledge that our behaviors are predetermined because we do not trust people, we do not trust ourselves, and we think that we cannot share our feelings. By owning our predetermined behavior, we set in motion absolute accountability, thereby creating access to the type of thinking, feeling, speaking, and perceiving that drives an extraordinary future full of possibility. In our seminar series, each participant is challenged to come to grips with the truth that people without self-awareness have no capacity to choose and therefore unintentionally generate all kinds of dysfunction in their lives: broken relationships, failed careers, and substance use disorder. However, we can embrace our innate ability to choose and create what we truly desire. Life is created by us; it is not happening to us.

Mind Dynamics's Life Skills Seminars focus on conscious creation; we explore how the individual has generated their results and can instead create a healthy, successful life. Our seminars address the key components that comprise an inspired life: self-care, healthy relationships, financial freedom, and mental and emotional health. Each class examines the ego positions that have generated past results. Some of these positions can overlap. For example, the ego often takes the position of scarcity as a way to access power and control, and that identity impacts our ability to create wealth and receive love. So, two distinctly different seminars on financial management and parenting will uncover the self's relationship to the same ego identity, "I believe good things are scarce." When we come from scarcity, we will lose all access to love and wealth, which means we cannot give or receive love and wealth. By taking complete responsibility for the quality of our life, we can begin to imagine, design, and achieve life extraordinary and sober. Each of us can transform our future.

Mind Dynamics utilizes the ACE Questionnaire to introduce the idea that childhood trauma is connected to behaviors that have sabotaged the participants' ability to achieve. Our approach is indirect because the seminar series is designed to be educational, not confrontational. We do not examine our participants' childhood in detail. Instead, we identify the ego identities that most people take in response to childhood trauma, like scarcity. We survey the behaviors associated with scarcity and the impact that those behaviors have on current results. Our seminars are designed to be supportive in nature. They are a steppingstone into deeper work.

The courses in the Life Skills Seminar Series are designed for those in recovery and their families. Graduates of our outpatient curriculum or others who have completed their fourth step are invited to participate and grow. If the participants do not meet these requirements, we will support them in creating a path that works. The choice to participate is grounded in the person's commitment to their personal transformation.

Empowerment Training

Basic Training is built on the principle that every human being has an unlimited reserve of possibility: anyone can transform their limitations and build a life extraordinary and sober. This profound three-day experience introduces participants to the ego-driven self: the person inside who has created an environment that tolerates disconnection, financial scarcity, and substance use disorder. Through participation in Basic Training, participants learn how to transform their relationship to the ego-driven self and become who they choose to be.

Advanced Training explores the possibility that exists out of taking a stand for transformation. While Basic Training introduces participants to their ego-driven selves, Advanced Training introduces a conversation, a process, and a way of being to bring personal transformation into the real world. We use language to define ourselves, and our *way of being* is the source of our results. By taking a stand for transformation, participants come face to face with their ego-driven way of being. Participants will be inspired to truly examine the world that they have built for the people they love. Graduates of Advanced Training understand how to develop a conversation that creates an environment that drives sobriety and life extraordinary.

Advanced Training Empowerment Series (Adv-ES) is a 90-day curriculum for graduates of Advanced Training. This training examines the amount of love, success, and connection that clients will allow into their lives. Participants confront their capacity to consciously create their life, and possibility is breathed into existence using language. For example, "I am raw potential, and I will take an unreasonable stand for transformation. I am not here to be liked or admired. Rather, I understand that I am dysfunctional, and I am committed to the transformation of myself and others." Adv-ES inspires families, peer-to-peer leaders, and people who choose recovery to live their transformation in the face of adversity. Participants learn how to relate to the ego-driven self while loving, accepting, and guiding it to build a life extraordinary and sober.

Conclusion

EVERYONE IN THE RECOVERY COMMUNITY CAN LEARN to leverage adversity and dramatically improve the quality of their lives. *Mind Dynamics* will accomplish its mission by teaching the recovery community how to embrace its creative nature. When our creative nature is neglected, we become depressed, anxious, and miserable. Human beings cannot live their lives feeling dead inside without suffering consequences. We can wait, delay, and try our best to reduce our creativity to almost nothing, but we cannot destroy our potential. We did not create ourselves, and we cannot abandon the essence of who we are. We were born out of the glory of a divinity that grants us all the freedom to create our lives. We will either develop our capacity to choose according to our innate potential, or we will spend our lives suffering as we manage the fears that stifle our creative expression. When our fear sabotages our capacity to be fully creative and alive, our lives will reflect this breakdown. We will continue to live with broken relationships, financial hardship, and behavioral health disorders.

Substance use disorder treatment approaches must provide access to personal transformation: each person in the recovery community must be taught how to move through their past pain and trauma and express their creative potential. The recovery community must shift its focus from solving the problems presented by the person who chooses recovery and address the dysfunctional environment that holds disease in place.

Mind Dynamics invites everyone in the recovery community to confront their emotional addiction by playing for personal and professional goals that challenge their existing barriers to performance. Each goal is an opportunity to explore self-imposed limitations and sets in motion a conversation that aligns with the transformation of the self, "I am not my ego. I am who I choose to be." Families can learn a new language of healing that builds an environment that inspires each member of the family to thrive in the face of adversity. Families will no longer enable emotional addiction; everyone will be inspired to confront their limitations.

Conventional treatment approaches feed dysfunction because they enable family members to hide their childhood trauma and avoid taking the emotional risk that inspires healing. People are not taught how to liberate themselves from emotional disease. The current cycle of substance abuse, treatment, relapse, and death keeps us from confronting ourselves. This environment is dysfunctional from the inside out, from inside the family to the outside in those who choose recovery.

Mind Dynamics expands the speaking and listening that occurs in conventional treatment to a bigger conversation where everyone in the family is confronted by their limitations. This leaves room for a new world of possibility to be created for everyone who participates.

No one would consciously choose substance use disorder and all the dysfunction and death that it brings to a family.

Substance use disorder is devastating for families. The disease ruins relationships and drives many other forms of abuse that become generational. Despite their suffering, families are not victims of substance use disorder; they are unintentionally generating an environment where substance use disorder can destroy their lives. Families are reacting to past pain rather than choosing to create consciously. No one would consciously choose substance use disorder and all the dysfunction and death that it brings. However, without developing self-awareness, families have no alternative but to generate an environment based on emotional reactions to unresolved past wounds. This unresolved pain usually has its roots in childhood trauma and is compounded by all of the misery associated with addiction.

Mind Dynamics invites families to develop their capacity to choose a new future and create an environment that produces an entire community of transformed people committed to life extraordinary and sober. Our seminar series and empowerment training produce families that can create connection, acceptance, and support for those who choose recovery. Families and peers learn how to set boundaries, develop emotional resilience, and integrate those in recovery back into healthy relationships.

Peer-to-peer interactions are crucial to the recovery process, but without experiencing the extraordinary themselves, peers have access to sobriety but not life extraordinary. Many peers are sober but suffer from depression and anxiety and feel dead inside. In a *Mind Dynamics* Sober Community, peers who have achieved life extraordinary and sober inspire others to create a new life. *Mind Dynamics* teaches peer-to-peer leaders how to develop emotional availability, engage in the conscious creation of their lives, and duplicate that transformation in others. Peer-to-peer interactions occur in educational groups that generate useful life skills rather than support groups that tolerate dysfunction. Transformed peers inspire those who choose recovery to leverage the power of absolute accountability, radical honesty, transparency, and emotional integrity.

The future is full of potential for those in recovery, their families, and their friends. Everyone in the recovery community has the opportunity to change the conversation about substance use disorder treatment from one that drives sobriety while sabotaging choice to one that inspires life extraordinary and sober. We must recognize our role in generating an environment that enables and tolerates the disease. We can break the generational pattern of addiction by choosing to create an environment that inspires those who choose recovery along with their family and peers to create what is truly possible in their lives.

Facilities can learn how to build an environment that confronts the individual's need for safety as they transform barriers into conscious creation. A *Mind Dynamics* Sober Community holds in place the value of sobriety and personal transformation. Participants actualize the power of absolute accountability, radical honesty, transparency, and emotional integrity. The love and connection that did not exist in the past are now the present reality, and sarcasm, hostility, and resentment are exchanged for listening and acceptance. Financial achievement begins to show up as families work together to achieve their goals. An environment is born that inspires the creative act instead of one that mutes emotional experiences. Families embrace a performance-oriented dynamic that highlights the creative power of authentic self-expression: the present moment becomes a new adventure as each individual examines the current framework that tolerates a cycle of abuse, treatment, relapse, and death. *Mind Dynamics* is committed to supporting the recovery community in the creative process to access the power of choice to achieve life extraordinary and sober.

Made in the USA
Middletown, DE
12 October 2023